Facts and ARTEFACTS

ANCIENT GREECE

Tim Cooke

W
FRANKLIN WATTS
LONDON • SYDNEY

Published in Great Britain in 2018 by
The Watts Publishing Group

Copyright © 2018 Brown Bear Books Ltd

For Brown Bear Books Ltd:
Managing Editor: Tim Cooke
Children's Publisher: Anne O'Daly
Editorial Director: Lindsey Lowe
Design Manager: Keith Davis
Designer and Illustrator: Supriya Sahai
Picture Manager: Sophie Mortimer

Concept development: Square and Circus/
Brown Bear Books Ltd

ISBN: 978 1 4451 6165 5

Printed in Malaysia

Franklin Watts
An imprint of
Hachette Children's Group
Part of the Watts Publishing Group
Carmelite House
50 Victoria Embankment
London EC4Y 0DZ

An Hachette UK company
www.hachette.co.uk
www.franklinwatts.co.uk

FSC
www.fsc.org
MIX
Paper from
responsible sources
FSC® C137506

Picture credits
Front Cover: istockphoto: fotoon, main; Public
Domain: Michel, Frederic, bottom, Staatliche
Antikensammlungen, top.
Interior: Alamy: Chronicle, 16–17; Dreamstime:
Lefteris, Papaulakis, 21t, Xioma, 7; istockphoto:
Pierre Delune, 6–7, A Eduard, 15b, fotoon, 10–11,
J Hayes, 24–25, MR1805, 8–9; Public Domain: 23,
Philipp Foltz, 12t, Michel Frederic, 9, Los Angeles
County Museum of Art, 13t, Musee de Louvre,
19, Museum of Fine Arts Lyon, 11, Staatliche
Antikensammlungen, 15t, Szilas/J.M. Roberts
East Asia and Classical Greece, 14–15, Vatican
Museum, 20–21, Onno, Zweers, 22–23;
Shutterstock: Alex Coan, 16b, ColoArt, 25br,
Dimitris_K, 12–13, Sergey Goryachev, 18t,
Kaband, 17t, Kamira, 1, 5, Panos Karas, 18–19, Todd
Kreykes, 4, Vasilis Ververidis, 25.
t=top, c=centre, b=bottom, l=left, r=right
All maps and other artwork Brown Bear Books.

Brown Bear Books have made every attempt to
contact the copyright holder.
If you have any information please contact:
licensing@brownbearbooks.co.uk

Websites
The website addresses (URLs) included in
this book were valid at the time of going to
press. However, it is possible that contents or
addresses may change following the publication
of this book. No responsibility for any such
changes can be accepted by either the author
or the publisher.

CONTENTS

ANCIENT GREECE

Ancient Greece is the name given to the civilisation of the Greek mainland and the islands of the Aegean Sea from about the ninth century BCE to the sixth century CE.

GREEK HISTORY

The highpoint of Greek civilisation was the classical period of the 500s and 400s BCE. Greece was divided into city-states, such as Athens, in which a city and its territory formed a political unit. Each state had its own leader, laws and economy. The Greek states sometimes fought against one another. At other times, they came together to fight common enemies, such as the Persian Empire.

Despite their political divisions, most Greeks spoke the same language, worshipped identical gods and enjoyed the same culture. Greek city-states such as Athens became wealthy. They were home to philosophers and playwrights. Athens led the development of democracy.

The ancient Greeks worshipped gods at temples like this one at Olympia, dedicated to the god Apollo.

ITALY

GREECE

Black Sea

ASIA MINOR

Athens

Mediterranean Sea

PERSIA

Aegean Sea

Ancient Greece

Crete

ARTEFACTS

The Greeks were skilled builders, craftspeople, artists and inventors. Many of the objects they made survive today, such as sculptures, paintings and pottery. One of the best ways to discover how the Greeks lived and how they thought is by studying these artefacts. These ancient objects enable us to step back into the world of the people who made them.

The ancient Greeks were famous for their pottery, which was often decorated with red and black designs., like this charioteer.

THE ROOTS OF ANCIENT GREECE

The Minoans on the island of Crete formed the first civilisation of ancient Greece. From about 2600 BCE, they began building large palaces. The Minoans traded with their neighbours in Egypt, Greece and what is now Turkey. The Minoan civilisation ended around 1100 BCE.

TURKEY

GREECE

Crete

☞ THE FACTS

- The Minoans were named after the legendary King Minos.
- According to Greek legend, Minos kept a creature called the Minotaur, who was half-man and half-bull, in a maze beneath his palace at Knossos.
- The Minoans made decorated pottery and were skilled at working with metals such as bronze.
- The Minoans had a system of writing, but no one has learned how to read it.

The storerooms beneath the palace at Knossos may have been the basis of the legend about the Minotaur's maze.

The largest Minoan palace was at Knossos in Crete. Its walls were decorated with brightly coloured paintings, or murals.

BULL-LEAPING FRESCO

Minoan religion was based on the worship of bulls. Bulls appear on the walls of the main palace at Knossos.

In some of the paintings, young men and women are leaping over the bodies of running bulls. This was very dangerous. It was probably part of a religious ritual. The bull might have been a symbol of fertility. The importance of the bull in Minoan life could be traced to the roots of the Greek myth of the Minotaur.

This painting from the palace at Knossos shows an athlete leaping over a charging bull.

THE TROJAN WARS

In the 700s BCE, the poet Homer composed a poem called *The Illiad*. It told how Greek warriors had fought against the city of Troy. Most people thought the story was a legend. Then, in the 1880s, archeologists found the ruins of Troy in modern-day Turkey.

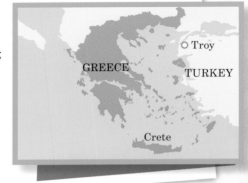

GREECE
Troy
TURKEY
Crete

Wooden Horse After 10 years, the Greeks pretended to leave, but left behind a large model of a horse as a gift for the gods. This is a modern artist's idea of what the horse looked like.

☞ THE FACTS

The Trojan Wars began when a prince from Troy stole Helen, wife of the Greek ruler Menelaus. According to Homer, Greek rulers and their warriors sailed to Troy in Asia Minor to punish the Trojans. They besieged the city for 10 years. Then, they used a trick (see main image) to defeat the Trojans and burned the city. The ruins of Troy show that it had been destroyed by fire – just as Homer's poem described.

When the Trojans took the wooden horse into the city, Greek warriors hidden inside opened the city gates. Greek armies came in and captured and burned the city.

THE GOLD MASK

This gold mask was made about 3,500 years ago. It was found in the tomb of a warrior in the ancient kingdom of Mycenae in Greece.

Mycenae was powerful at about the time of the Trojan Wars in the 1200s BCE. When the mask was discovered in 1876, archeologists claimed that it showed the face of King Agamemnon, who led the Greek forces in the wars against Troy. Today, most experts do not believe the mask shows the face of Agamemnon. It dates from before the time when Agamemnon is thought to have lived.

THE CLASSICAL AGE

By the 700s BCE, the Greek mainland and islands were divided among dozens of city-states. These city-states often worked together in a series of shifting alliances. The richest and most powerful city-state was Athens.

GREECE

TURKEY

Athens

☞ THE FACTS

Athens became wealthy thanks to trade. It had a powerful navy that protected Athenian cargo ships as they carried goods throughout the Aegean Sea. Athenian leaders used the wealth from trade to build spectacular temples and public buildings. From the 600s BCE, Athens led many developments in Greek politics and ideas.

Acropolis The Athenians built a series of temples and other buildings on this high rock named the Acropolis.

Parthenon The largest building on the Acropolis was the Parthenon. This temple was dedicated to Athena, the main goddess of the city.

SYMBOL OF ATHENA

The Athenians named their city after Athena, the Greek goddess of wisdom.

They believed that the goddess protected the city, so they were careful to worship her devoutly. The Parthenon held a huge statue of Athena covered in gold that reflected the sunlight. Athena's symbol was the owl, which appeared on Athenian coins.

The ancient Greeks stamped symbols on their coins to identify where they came from.

THE BIRTH OF DEMOCRACY

Athens is often called the first democracy in the world. In the sixth century BCE, Athenians began to gather on the Acropolis to debate key issues of the day.

Athenians gather on the Acropolis. Only male citizens were allowed to vote.

☞ THE FACTS

- In the early 500s BCE, the Athenian ruler Solon introduced an assembly that included all male citizens.
- The assembly met forty times a year to vote on new laws.
- Women, slaves and male non-citizens (men not born in Athens) were not allowed to vote.
- Citizens could only vote on laws put forward by the aristocrats, who held the real power in Athens.

OSTRACON

Most votes were taken by a show of hands. However, when Athenians voted to banish someone from the city as a punishment, there was a secret vote.

The voters scratched their decision on pieces of broken pottery, which were then counted. Broken pots were easy to find. The pieces were called *ostraca*. The word led to the modern word 'ostracise', which means to exclude someone from society.

Voters could write their opinion on an ostracon as well as their decision.

Athenians met to debate and vote at this rocky outcrop on the Acropolis.

GREEKS AT WAR

The Greek city-states were often at war. They fought one another to gain land or to increase their trade. At times, they came together to fight a common enemy. In the 600s BCE, Greek armies defeated invasions by the Persian Empire.

GREECE

PERSIAN EMPIRE

INDIA

AFRICA

Greek warriors were known as hoplites. They fought in rows with round shields and spears.

☞ THE FACTS

- The Greeks fought against Persia in the 600s BCE. There were major conflicts between Greek states in the 400s and 300s BCE.
- At sea, the Greeks used long warships powered by many rowers.

- Sparta was the most warlike city-state. It took young boys from their families to train as warriors.
- Spartan boys were raised in barracks and taught to live and fight in harsh conditions.

HELMET

Hoplites wore armour that included a bronze helmet and a bronze or leather breastplate. They carried a small round shield.

Hoplites were armed with long spears and short swords. They usually fought hand-to-hand, and the Greeks celebrated displays of personal bravery in such fighting. By the 500s BCE, the hoplites were being replaced by javelin throwers and archers. Some armies also used cavalry to launch devastating raids on the enemy.

The warrior on this plate has a shield and a short sword for stabbing.

A hoplite helmet had a crest to protect the top of the head from sword blows.

The Greeks prized displays of individual courage in hand-to-hand fighting on the battlefield.

TRADE

City-states such as Athens gained their wealth from trade. They traded food and other resources with one another. Greek ships also carried goods between the Greek islands and around the shores of the Mediterranean and Black Seas.

From around 600 BCE, Greek traders began to use cargo ships to carry goods.

These coins were made by different city-states.

AMPHORA

Pottery vessels called amphorae were used to transport and store liquids, including wine and olive oil, or dry goods, such as grains.

One of the most important Greek commodities was the olive. Olive trees grew well even in dry, poor soil. Olives were used as food, but they were also a source of olive oil. The oil was used for cooking and for skincare. It was also burned in lamps.

This amphora was recovered from an ancient shipwreck. It was designed to be easy to store and carry.

Banks of rowers and square sails enabled Greek ships to travel quickly.

 THE FACTS

- The Greeks exported wine and olives, as well as grains and pottery.
- Goods imported to the Greek mainland and islands included cereals, gold and silver, and spices.
- The Athenians built a railway to carry goods on tracks across a narrow neck of land between two seas at Corinth, in the south of the Greek mainland.
- Trade increased as Greeks set up colonies around the Mediterranean.
- The Greeks developed a system of coinage to facilitate trade.

GREEK GODS

The Greeks worshipped many gods and goddesses, such as Apollo, the god of music, and Ares, the god of war. They thought of the main gods as a human family, who often argued with each other.

Hera was queen of the gods and the goddess of women.

☞ THE FACTS

- The most important gods were the twelve Olympian gods, who were ruled by Zeus and his queen, Hera.
- It was believed that the gods sometimes wandered the earth and interfered in human affairs.
- Greeks performed rituals in temples, made offerings and prayed for the gods' help.
- According to legend, Greek gods and goddesses had children with mortals. The children were demigods with special gifts.

The Greeks believed the most important gods lived on top of Mount Olympus, this tall mountain in northern Greece.

ZEUS STATUE

Greek artists portrayed gods and goddesses with symbols that helped people recognise them.

Zeus, king of the gods – **lightning bolt**

Hera, queen of the gods – **peacock**

Poseidon, god of the sea – **trident**

Hades, god of the Underworld – **pomegranate**

Hestia, goddess of the home – **fireplace**

Athena, goddess of wisdom – **owl**

Artemis, goddess of the moon – **moon**

Apollo, god of music – **lyre**

Aphrodite, goddess of love – **dove**

Hephaestus, god of fire – **hammer**

Ares, god of war – **dog**

Hermes, messenger of the gods – **rod entwined with serpents**

This statue of Zeus was discovered in Turkey in 1680. It shows Zeus holding a lightning bolt to hurl against his enemies.

CLASSICAL THINKING

From the 600s BCE, some Greeks began to try to explain the world using reason, rather than seeing events as the actions of the gods. This approach is called philosophy. The Greeks were some of the most influential philosophers in history.

Plato's teachings were written down by his students, so they have survived for 2,400 years.

👉 THE FACTS

Athens was the centre of what became known as classical Greek philosophy. The city's first famous classical philosopher was Socrates, who laid the foundations for Western philosophy in the 400s BCE. In the following century, Plato established an academy in Athens to teach philosophy. One of his pupils was Aristotle, who became tutor to Alexander the Great.

GREEK ALPHABET

The Greeks developed their own alphabet around the 900s BCE. Students of the Greek philosophers wrote down the teachings of their masters.

The invention of writing helped the Greeks preserve and share knowledge. They were interested not only in practical subjects but also in abstract ideas such as truth and justice. Subjects such as logic were considered an important part of the education of leading citizens.

This stone tablet is carved with the Greek alphabet, which had 24 letters.

Plato's student Aristotle helped begin the study of physical and natural sciences.

The School of Athens (1509—1511) was painted by the Italian artist Raphael. It shows an imaginary gathering of the leading philosophers from ancient Greece.

GREEK DRAMA

Going to the theatre was a popular pastime in ancient Greece. Most towns had large, open-air theatres. The action took place on a flat area called the orchestra. Scenery was erected behind the actors. It is not known if women went to performances. Some modern experts believe that only men were allowed to attend.

☞ THE FACTS

There were two types of Greek theatre: tragedy and comedy. Tragedies were usually based on stories from Greek mythology. They showed heroes stuck in difficult situations and explored ideas about right and wrong behaviour. Leading writers of tragedies included Aeschlyus, Sophocles and Euripides. Comedies were more often about current events. They included satirical comments about politicians and other citizens. The leading comedy writers were Aristophanes and Menander.

Buildings behind the orchestra served as scenery or allowed actors to change costume.

THEATRE MASKS

All performers in Greek plays were male. Only three performers spoke in any play.

The three actors wore masks to allow them to play a number of roles in the play. The masks also helped indicate the different characters the actors were playing, especially for spectators a long way from the orchestra. The actors were accompanied by a chorus, or group of people. In both tragedies and comedies the chorus danced and sang, but in comedies the chorus had the additional function of commenting on the action as it took place.

This mask was worn by an actor portraying Zeus, the king of the gods.

Greek theatres like this one at Dodona were built for excellent acoustics, so that everyone could hear.

THE OLYMPIC GAMES

In 776 BCE, Greek athletes gathered at Olympia to hold a running race in honour of Zeus. From then on, games were held at Olympia every four years. Each period of four years was called an Olympiad. Athletes from all over Greece came to compete in the games.

GREECE

Olympia

☞ THE FACTS

- The games were hosted by the city of Elis. Up to 45,000 spectators attended the games.
- Women were not allowed to watch the events.
- Leading up to the games, all wars stopped in Greece so that people could travel to Elis.
- The games were held every four years from 776 BCE to CE 393 – a run of 293 Olympiads.

The oldest event was the stadion, a race over a stadium track 192 metres long.

DISCUS THROWER

The Olympics grew from a single running race to include 18 events held over five days.

Many events were related to skills used by warriors, such as wrestling and javelin throwing. The winners were awarded a crown of olive leaves. The victors became famous throughout Greece. The winner of the stadion gave his name to the whole Olympiad.

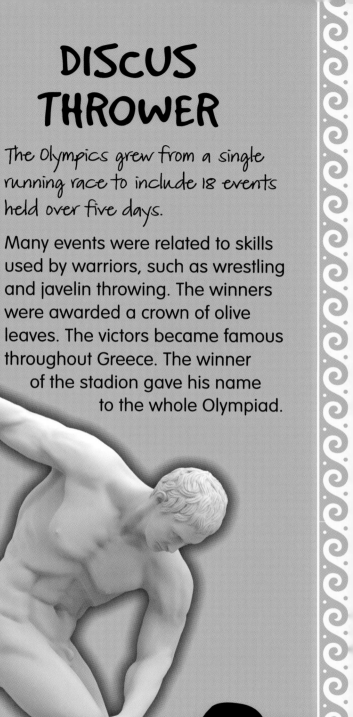

Ceremonial temples and avenues were built at the site of the games.

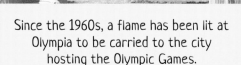

Since the 1960s, a flame has been lit at Olympia to be carried to the city hosting the Olympic Games.

The Discobolus was carved around 450 BCE. It shows an athlete throwing a discus.

PERSEUS AND MEDUSA

Just as artefacts tell us a lot about cultures from the past, the stories people told reveal what they thought about their world. Most ancient cultures used myths to explain their beliefs. Many Greek myths featured good triumphing over evil.

A carving of a Gorgon created in around 580 BCE.

Perseus was the son of Zeus and a beautiful princess named Danaë. Danaë's father banished her and her son to the kingdom of Polydectes. Perseus grew up brave and strong. He protected his mother from the unwelcome attention of Polydectes. The king decided to get Perseus out of the way. He ordered the young man to bring him the head of Medusa. She was one of the three Gorgons, terrible monsters with long claws and teeth like boars' claws. Instead of hair, Medusa's head was covered in hissing serpents. Anyone who looked at a Gorgon's face was turned to stone.

It seemed that Perseus was doomed. Getting close to Medusa was impossible. But Athena and her half-brother, Hermes the messenger god, decided to help. They gave Perseus gifts to help him with his quest.

Hermes lent Perseus a pair of winged sandals that enabled him to fly, a helmet that made the wearer invisible, a sickle and a magic bag. Athena gave the young man a special shield. Its surface had been polished so much that it was like a mirror. She told Perseus he could use the shield to look at Medusa's reflection without being harmed. Perseus took the gifts and flew to the edge of the world, where Medusa lived. The approach to her lair was lined by the figures of heroes she had turned to stone.

As Perseus grew closer, the monster attacked him with an angry hissing sound. Perseus raised his shield so that he could only see Medusa's reflection. Then he swung his sickle and cut off her head. The head still had the power to turn people to stone, so he put it inside the magic bag. Then he flew back home to present his trophy to the king and save his mother.

TIMELINE OF ANCIENT GREECE

1100 BCE
The Minoan civilisation is destroyed by the eruption of a volcano at Thera.

c.2600 BCE
The Minoan civilisation begins on Crete.

900s BCE
The Greek alphabet begins to develop.

c.700 BCE
Around now the poet Homer – or a group of poets – write the long poems *The Illiad* and the *Odyssey*.

2600 BCE

1100s BCE

600s BCE

c.1260 BCE
The Trojan Wars may have taken place at around this time.

776 BCE
The first Olympic Games are held in honour of the god Zeus.

508 BCE
Citizens in Athens get the right to vote. This is the beginning of democracy.

c.700 BCE
By now Greek cities are founding colonies in Asia Minor and around the Mediterranean Sea.

470s BCE
Greek theatre becomes popular in Athens.

338 BCE
Philip of Macedon takes control of Greece.

c.500 BCE
The classical age of Athens begins around this time.

404 BCE
After nearly thirty years of fighting, Athens is defeated by Sparta in the Pelopponesian War.

336 BCE
Alexander the Great becomes ruler of Greece.

500s BCE

300s BCE

100s BCE

490 BCE
Greek armies defeat a Persian invasion at the Battle of Marathon.

432 BCE
Building of the Parthenon is completed in Athens.

146 BCE
Greece falls under the control of the Roman Empire. This marks the end of ancient Greece.

399 BCE
Death of Socrates, the founder of modern philosophy.

460 BCE
Hippocrates, the father of modern medicine, is born around now.

GLOSSARY

abstract something that exists as an idea rather than as a physical object

acoustics the quality of sound transmission in a particular place

alliances unions formed by groups or people for mutual benefit

aristocrats members of a social class who inherit a privileged position in society

assembly a group of people who are gathered together for a particular purpose

barracks buildings used to house soldiers

besieged surrounded a location in order to force it to surrender

cargo ships vessels that carry goods for trade

cavalry soldiers who fight on horseback

citizens people with the right to vote in a particular place

classical relating to a high point of Greek or Roman tradition

colonies settlements founded by a country in other lands

commodities agicultural produce and raw materials that are traded

demigods beings who are half-divine and half-mortal

democracy a system of government in which citizens elect people to represent them in a parliament or assembly

fertility the ability of animals or plants to reproduce easily

javelin a long, light spear used for throwing

legendary someone famous about whom many stories are told

logic a way of thinking that is based on strict rules to decide whether or not an argument is valid

philosophers people who think about difficult questions such as the nature of reality or the meaning of existence

raids quick, small-scale attacks on a target, usually to seize goods

ritual a solemn ceremony that follows a series of actions

satirical revealing or mocking weak or foolish behaviour in a humorous way

sickle a tool with a curved blade used for cutting grain

FURTHER RESOURCES

Books

Writing History Ancient Greeks, Anita Ganeri
(Franklin Watts, 2017)

At Home with the Ancient Greeks, Tim Cooke
(Wayland, 2016)

Technology in the Ancient World Ancient Greece, Charlie Samuels
(Franklin Watts, 2015)

Ancient Greece
(Dorling Kindersley, 2014)

A Visitor's Guide to Ancient Greece, Lesley Sims
(Usborne, 2014)

Websites

**www.bbc.co.uk/schools/primaryhistory/
ancient_greeks/greek_world/**
This BBC site has information about ancient Greece
for primary school students.

**www.childrensuniversity.manchester.ac.uk/interactives/
history/greece/**
The Children's University of Manchester has an interactive site
with different topics about ancient Greece.

**www.natgeokids.com/uk/discover/history/greece/
10-facts-about-the-ancient-greeks/**
National Geographic Kids has a list of 10 fun facts
about the ancient Greeks.

www.primaryhomeworkhelp.co.uk
Click on the section on ancient Greece to find information
about ancient Greece and the ancient Greeks.

INDEX